Stop That!

Written by Maryann Dobeck

Illustrated by Don Madden

Two little pigs did a jig.

"Stop that!" said the cat.

Two little pigs put on wigs.

"Stop that!" said the cat.

Two little pigs began to dig.

"Stop that!" said the cat.

"Scat, cat!" said the pigs.

And she did.